THE RHYMES AND RUNES OF THE TOAD

Other books by Susan Fromberg Schaeffer

POETRY

The Witch and the Weather Report

Granite Lady

FICTION

Falling

Anya

The Rhymes and Runes of the Toad

Susan Fromberg Schaeffer

Illustrations by Sebastian Fleuret

Macmillan Publishing Co., Inc.
New York
Collier Macmillan Publishers
London

811
5

Macmillan Publishing Co., Inc.
866 Third Avenue, New York, N. Y. 10022
Collier Macmillan Canada, Ltd.

Library of Congress Cataloging in Publication Data
Schaeffer, Susan Fromberg.
 The rhymes and runes of the toad.
 I. Title.
PS3569.C35R5   811'.5'4   75-15927
ISBN 0-02-607040-5

First Printing 1975

Printed in the United States of America

 "The Toad Who Wanted to Be King" is reprinted from
Prairie Schooner. Copyright © 1972 by the University
of Nebraska Press.
 "Cornerstone Toad" and "Footstool Toad" are
reprinted from *Greenfield Review.*

For Judith Shaw

CONTENTS

Rhymes

The Song of the Toad

Everyone knows about the song of the toad,
How he sits on green lily leaves
And puffs himself up,
Singing, *croak! croak!*

There are legends about this.
Some people claim this is why
Earmuffs are muffling our ears,
Others that this is the reason

Butterflies cover their ears
With their wings,
But, as is the case with everything,
There is a story behind this.

Once, the toad sat on the rocks
And sang such beautiful tunes
Ships came to see him and hear him
And didn't hear the surf on the cliffs,

And hit them and drowned.
But as luck would have it,
A beautiful lady swam out of the sea
And kissed him *good*.

He turned, of course, as everyone knows,
Right into a prince.
"I will give you everything I have,"
Said the prince to the lady.

He was so happy
His eyes were stinging with salt.
But time kept passing, and finally
The prince began missing his mosses and rocks,

And, as so often happens,
He and the princess decided to part.
"Then I will have your voice,"
She said, and took it,

And swam to the land,
And multiplied, and after,
Generations called her Eve.
But this is not the end of the story yet.

The toad had a twin brother
Who fell in love with a tree.
The tree could not sing at all,
Just rattle her branches,

Like an axe chopping wood.
The toad's twin brother
Also began to be lonesome
For the mosses of the sea

And the emerald waves
Crowned always with pearl.
He said good-bye to the tree
Who was named Eloise,

But before he left,
He planted his tongue
In the ground near her feet.
There it took root, and grew

And was green as the waves
Of the sea, and soon
It covered the earth,
And waved in the wind

And people called it grass.
And on very dark nights
All these tongues start to sing
To their mother, the moon,

And their song
Is more delicate than lace
And more fragile than glass
And all the animals come

Down to the edge of the woods
And dance with the trees
And bow down to the plains
And catch hold of the songs

In their mouths and their paws.

The Old Woman Toad

Love is hard to find
And harder to keep.
There was an old woman
Who lost her love

As surely and finally
As coins falling out
Of a hole in her purse.
She lived alone

On the outskirts of town
Cleaning her house
And sometimes, if she stared
Into her pots

The scouring scratches
Would form into his face.
Then she would cook in it,
And eat,

And she would not be alone.
She had heard that her husband
Was the toad of the hill,
And she believed this so firmly

She mottled her hands
Into toadskin
To be always near him
And it is said

When she died
He came for her
And carried her off on his back
Before even the doctor could come.

Cornerstone Toad

Once it was thought that the toad
Had gone for good.

No more were the forests
Desecrated by his croak,

No more did the lily pads
Sink under his weight,

The fiddling cricket rejoiced,
He had come into his own at last.

The starling squawked with impunity
And you could almost hear the fireflies

Switching their lights on and off.
Of course, it occurred to no one

To look in the cities.
The toad had heard tales

And he knew where he was needed.
He consulted the witch of the borough

And she gave him a cloak
And she told him if he put it on

His shoulders, it would open a door
To each and every cornerstone in the town!

This the toad did.
And when he got in,

He read all the old papers and scrolls,
He studied all the utensils,

The pictures, the knives, and the forks.
Then he waved his magic cloak

And a tiny window appeared in the wall.
Then toad got down to work

And began to observe.
He sat at a table, and began taking notes.

Think twice when you think
You hear the croak of a bus or a truck.

Toad is taking note
Of your feet as you pass.

He knows everything that you do.
Everything you own rests on his stone.

And the trees, and the moon, and the cliffs
Are waiting for his report.

Earring Toad

There was a saying
Toad knew too much
He was too full of himself.
He was puffed up like a cloud.

Man bought him a one-way ticket
To the land of the stone,
The deaf stone, and the bog.
Woman, however, knew better,

Suspected something, and followed.
''Tell me everything,'' she said,
But toad had his conditions.
Woman returned

With a hole in each ear,
And dangling from a gold wire
In each ear
Was a small golden toad.

Now man grows nervous
When woman stares off into space
Conversing, apparently,
With only herself.

Astronaut Toad

There once was a very young toad
Who stayed in his room
Where the rays of light slid in
Most brightly,

And did nothing but read.
His mother, who believed
In the great green outdoors,
Grew frantic. ''The chameleon

Has changed his colors thirteen times,
And still you do nothing but read.''
Her son was unimpressed,
And would not even look up.

''Your eyes will fall out of your head,''
She said, for, considering
The normal look of a toad,
This was the worst insult

She could think up.
Her son sighed, closed his book,
And went out. By this time,
It was night, and the chameleon

Was dressed up in black
And was nowhere to be seen.
The next day, Toad's mother came in
With a smile, and a weather report,

And an egg on a plate.
But Toad was pawing the pages
Of his book like a jeweller
Searching a gem.

"What now?" said his mother,
Goggling her eyes, which indeed
Appeared about to fall out.
"I want to go to the moon,"

He said. "I saw it last night.
It is white as an egg. Sometimes,
It is silver, like a coin."
Toad was eagerly reading

In a section called "m,"
But soon he hopped eagerly out.
"Toads cannot climb trees,"
His mother said sternly

When she found him later,
And again, when she found him
Bargaining with a spider for his web.
"Neither are toads acrobats,"

Said his mother, when she found him
On the shoulders of three gloomy toads
From his fourth period class.
"You are not a pogo stick,"

She informed him
When she caught him
Leaping rhythmically into the air
Like a small ping-pong ball.

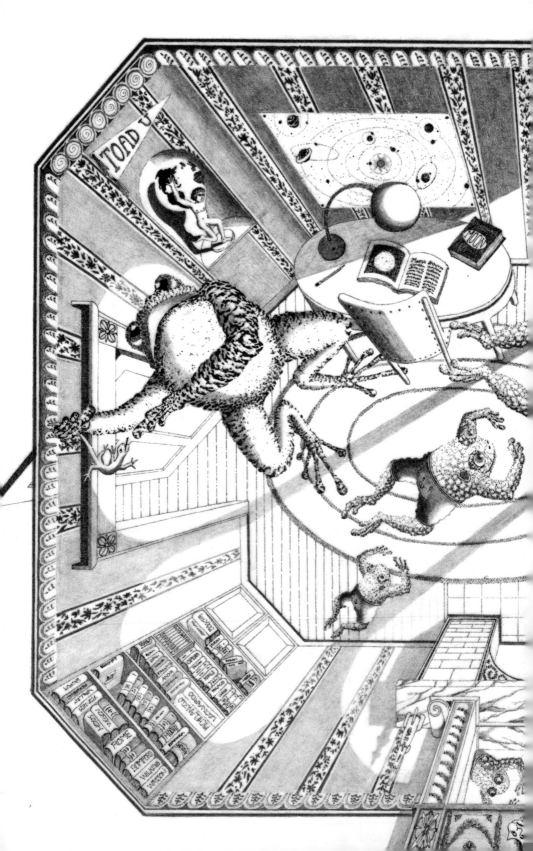

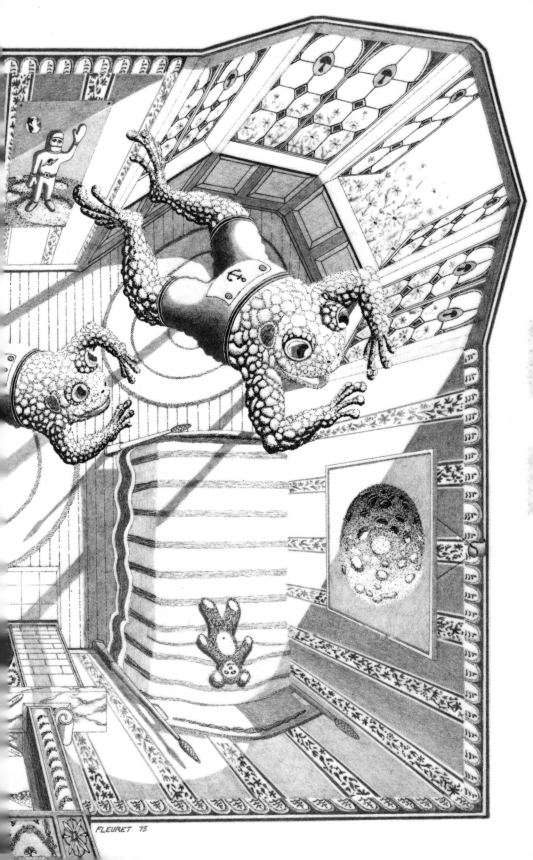

FLEURET 75

"The Great Toad of Surinaam
Is not interested in the moon,
Nor does she take
Travelers on her back,"

Said his mother
When she came upon him
Hopefully goggling the globe.
Toad grew depressed,

And lay on his back
For a day and a night.
His mother decided to send him
Down to the river and the duck

Who was said to be wondrously wise.
Then Toad had his hopes up,
And asked all about wings.
The duck quacked

It could not be done
In that way, but told him
To come back when the moon
Was as full as a plate.

Toad watched the moon
Pulling through the thin slot
In the sky, and when it came
Entirely loose,

He hopped down to the marsh.
There in the river,
The moon was bathing like a queen
With her attendants of rays.

Toad was struck dumb. "Now watch,"
Said the duck, "for your feet
Also are webbed,"
And he dove right in

And little silver beads rose up
Into the black air like stars.
Then Toad dived in like a swan
And when he came out

He was slippery and shiny
As the slippery moon
"O it will come off in the morning,"

He said to himself,
And bowed to the duck, and hopped
Happily home, nodding politely
To every leaf as it shook,

And every shadow that slithered.
But it did not come off,
And in the morning,
Toad found he was silver,

And very changeable,
And knew things
That were never in books
And could speak

In a handful of tongues.
His mother was very puzzled,
But for some reason,
Not really upset,

And busied herself setting
Out coffee and tea cakes and tea
For her numerous, goggling
And apparently permanent

River of guests.

Paternal Toad

Finally, Toad had children.
Toad took fatherhood very seriously,
Especially since, being a toad,
He had hundreds of them.

One cold afternoon in the fall
When the leaves were beginning
To whirl, and the ponds were lacing
With ice, he called them all

To him. He took his place
Upon a rock, and they sat down below,
Leaf green and gray,
Leaf green and beige.

"It is time for me to tell you
How the world came to begin,"
Said Toad. "First, there was blackness,
Then a red ball of fire

Rose in the sky, then darkness again,
Then a white ball of fire,
Not nearly so hot,
And so the pattern was set."

"What happened next?" they chorused,
Their minds all agog.
At this,
Toad threw himself down on his rock

And sobbed himself sick.

Fiery Toad

The toad is always cold
But he is not always ugly.
Sometimes he covers himself

Over with valuable stones,
And gold, and precious jewels,
And even his little feet

Are covered in silver mesh.
Wearing this dress,
He can hop right into a fire

And not burn up at all.
When he is glowing red hot
He can grant whatever wishes

You want
But you must be careful
Not to drop him

Or he will fall through the earth
Like a stone
Straight through to China

And rise in their sky like a sun
While the light goes out
Forever in your own.

FLEURET 1915

Footstool Toad

There is a legend
The whole world rests on a toad.

Grown-ups claim this is why
There are earthquakes, and fires,

And high tides, and low tides,
Because, as everyone knows,

A toad always jumps;
He jumps past the sun,

He jumps past the moon,
He jumps out of light into dark.

He will never stay put.
Adults do not like this at all.

The toad, however, likes
Jumping from one black glass pond

To another black glass pond.
And because the children like

The sensation of the stomach
Rising, then falling,

Like a sled going over the top,
Nothing can ever be done.

Guru Toad

The wisest person in the land
Was an ancient toad
Who lived on the very top
Of a sheer mountain of ice.

His skin was more wrinkled
Than tree skin, and it was said
He knew the language of leaves
And could talk to them with their tongues

And that each spire of his seven-spired crown
Held the wisdom of a great civilization
Many years gone.
From his throne at the top

Of his blue mountain of ice
He could see the people below
Trying, as they had been trying for years,
To reach him at the top.

They tried everything,
Shouting through cones of paper,
Standing on each other's shoulders,
Scaling the mountains like tendrils of flesh,

Coming in mountaineer suits
With acetylene picks;
They tried carrier pigeons.
They came back, afraid of the height.

One year, all the villagers
Painted their questions on rooftops,
Or arranged their radishes and potatoes
Into letters,

But toad's eyes had grown weak,
Or else, he would not reply.
He kept watching, and thinking,
And wrinkling, and each wrinkle

Held solutions to problems,
And answers to questions,
And cures for disease.
But most of all, he was waiting.

One day, a stranger came into the town
And took note of the people,
Their climbings and plottings,
And shook his big head.

He went to the other side of the mountain
Where the fields stretched out
And lay down before the violet sky.
He sat down near the mountain

And stared at his face in the ice.
Then toad began to stir,
And take interest.
The man sat there,

And stared at his face.
He hardly ate. He stared and stared.
He knew every wrinkle in his cheek,
And his eyes followed them

FLEURET '75

Like roads on a map.
On the third day, his eyes opened
Like doors.
"So that's it!" he cried. "That's the answer!"

Then toad stepped down from his throne
And slid down the mountain of ice
Like a child on a slide
And when he came to the bottom

He gave the man his seven-spired crown.
"You know," said the toad,
"I feel younger already,"
And went hopping off to the glade.

The man wore the crown
And sat down at the base
Of the mirrory mountain
And looked into it for hours,

And when he had taught the others
To do the same thing
The mountain began melting and melting
And occasionally, at night,

There is the croak of the old toad
Who sounds exceptionally happy
And the wrinkling man
With the crown of seven-spires

Is held in highest honor
And thought the wisest man in the land.

Businessman Toad

Everyone knows how the toad
Loves beautiful things,
How he will hop for a mile
To lie on a red scarf of silk,

His *frissons* of pleasure
When he sees golden balls
Falling and falling, into a well,
And how he will hop in

To get it, regardless of grub worms,
Or spiders, or tarantulas,
Or trolls. As we know from *Minute*
And *Monde*, his own home

Has walls solid with gold,
Ebony floors, ceilings of jewels—
No gingerbread castles for him!
Great crystal chandeliers

Cast prisms and unicorn horns
On the floor,
And he has tapestries of princesses,
Dancing, and tapestries of boars,
Fleeing, and no seat

Less intricately carved than a throne.
O any animal in the wood
Would feel it an honor
To be invited into the pictures

Of *Minute* and *Monde.*
Of course, a place of such splendor
Is hard to keep up,
So toad has turned himself into

The litterbag of the globe,
No job is too small for him,
He will go down sinks and drains,
And gutters and spouts,

You will hear him at night
Rattling trash cans and lids
You can see him through windows
In a light purplish-blue

Drawing blood out of bodies
Gone blue from the cold,
Painting on smiles.
You can find him sewing back arms,

Stamping ''approved''
On rubber elbows and knees
And it is him whom you call
To identify the fillings and rings

Left in the chars.
It is his voice that you hear
In the sirens of cars,
And, of course, in the foghorn's dull croak.

Morning always finds him
Tucked tight in his bed
Under covers of silk
And the sun strikes his tea things

Like small silver bells.
The toad
Is the true capitalist of the globe.

Housewife Toad

There was an old mother toad
Who lived under the roots
Of a great oak, whose brown ceilings
Vaulted above her,

And she scrubbed at their gnarls
And made war against ants
And had carpeted her floors
In the bright leaves of autumn

And even hung checked curtains
Over a window made where the clear sap
Welled, and there she set up
Her sink, and washed dish after dish

While she looked out at the forest
Made stranger and stranger
By the bubbly glass.
Every year her children set off

In the hundreds, their things
Tied up in checked cloth
Like curtains, and she would stand
In the leaf dust and wave,

While the sun hung above
Like a great golden tear
And as the children reached the place
Where the road bent,

They would always turn back
And wave one last time,
And she would wave one last time,
And wipe her hands on her apron,

And turn around and go in.
Finally, they were all gone,
And her husband, who had worked hard,
And was known in every hollow

As the best toadsuiter in the woods,
Was gone, and she was alone,
And would stand for hours
In front of the windows,

And it was rumored
She saw some very strange things.
One day, she saw her husband
Carrying all of his things

Wrapped in a bundle of red-checked cloth
Attached to a stick, and seven or eight
Of her children, all similarly equipped.
She stepped out of the window

To join him, and smiled when she saw
She had a bundle and stick
And her apron was gone,
And her cap was gone,

And they set off down the road.
Then they heard voices behind them,
And turned
And saw hundreds and hundreds

Of children behind them,
Waving and smiling,
And the sun hung in the sky
Like a golden toad smiling

And they reached a bend in the road
And were gone.

The Little Child's Toad

There was a child
Who met a toad
In a hole in a tree.

''Toad, come with me,''
He said,
''And I will show you the world.''

He showed the toad
Buildings, and skyscrapers,
And roller coasters, and movies,

And cookies, and ladies,
And department store hats.
The toad boggled his eyes

To show he was grateful
And let the child ride on his back
While he flew like a carpet.

He gave the child treasures,
And crowns, and jewels,
And finally a princess.

Then the child began to be afraid
He would lose the toad
Who did not sit well with grown-ups:

"Cold, ugly thing," they said.
So he swallowed it.
Then the toad was happier than a toad.

He began to tell the boy
Wonderful tales of the ruby caverns
Pulsing with blood,

And the white islands that float,
And the subways subterranean
In the stomach and blood.

Then the adults began tearing their hair
In fear for love of the toad
The child would turn himself inside out

And never again be seen
In the land.

Narcissus Toad

There was a time when toad
Was only 2,000 years old
And the world was only 2,000 years old,
And there were not even

Trees, or grass, or animals,
Only ashy, gray fields,
And blank, mirrory ponds.
Whenever toad passed one of these ponds

He would plunk himself down
And call out, ''Earth,
Let us celebrate a birthday,
For though you are large, and round,

I am beautiful, and a wonder,
And can walk where I please.''
Then the winds would rustle
As if giving assent

And toad agreed with himself
That these days were good.
Gradually, the earth became greener
And columns stood on it

And things moved in the shadows
But toad barely noticed
Because he was busy taking note of himself
Who could go where he pleased.

FLEURET 1975

One day, he looked into a pond, and there
Was something just like him,
But bigger, and made out of jade.
"And who are you, and what do you think!"

Demanded toad in a rage.
"I am frog," the creature answered,
And bigger than you, and may swim,
And may go where I please."

Toad felt totally wounded.
He called up his old friends,
The winds, and they called up the tides,
Frog called up his new friends,

The clouds, and soon the new leaves
Of the trees were rustling and rustling.
"Stop this," said the World,
"Or there will be a terrible storm."

But they would not stop
And puffed up their cheeks
Like storm clouds, and the storm tides
Swelled and swelled and covered the earth.

On the third day, frog,
Feeling triumphant,
Took time off from his frog kick
To wave with a leg

To an ark sailing placidly by,
But the two little toads,
Hidden in the hold
Between the sacks full of barley

Kept perfectly still.

Cloud Toad

A long time ago,
Before toad even had a shape,
God asked him what he would want to be like.

"Well," said toad, "I would like to be
Mottled, like the face of the heavens,
And I have fallen in love with the sun,

And would like to follow her
All through the sky."
God frowned and was puzzled

But toad drew a picture of himself
(Just as we know him)
And said, "Make me out of cloud,"

"I fear you are greedy," said God,
But I will do as you wish, for I asked you,"
And He created a great cloudy toad.

Toad was as pleased as a pickle.
Then God began to puff His cheeks, and blow.
"What are you thinking of?" shrieked toad

All alarmed. "Only what I must, if you
Are to follow the sun," said God.
Then toad felt a horrible shock.

His little feet were turning to claws,
His double chin to jaws,
Birds were fleeing from him in fright.

"Help!" shrieked the toad.
His paws were turning to scales,
Fire flew from his mouth,

His great scaly tail was lashing the sky.
"O this is not it at all!" cried toad,

His great tears falling as rain.
"I am sorry to say," said God,

Puffing up His cheeks again,
"Your will has been done."

Runes

The Toad Who Wanted to Be King

Once upon a time, when Toad was looking in the river, he saw the light flickering over his head, golden, like a seven-spired crown, and decided this must mean something, this was a sign; he decided he would be King.

"Oh fish," he cried out, first casting three red leaves down the river, its waters leaping and diving like minnows of silver (for Toad was wise in the ways of the river, and knew the fish's great love of pomp). "O fish," he cried, "I would be King, I would be King!"

The green fish rose up in a circle of bubbles, standing like a column of jade on his silvery tail. "Then you must go to the edge of things," said the fish, "there where the crown hangs on a great gray hook, the great gray hook called *time*." "But how do I get to the edge of things?" cried Toad, puzzled and perplexed. "Do you mean the edge of the forest, where the trees thin out like old fur, and the ground is bare, and great animals rush by in a wind, honking like geese?" "No," said the fish, "To the edge of things, where the skies thin out, and the stars wait, their silver spikes stretched out like arms; where the stars wait, seven-spired, like great silver crowns." "But how do I get there?" asked Toad, seeing a road stretching out like the wide beams of light the moon casts on the river, picturing himself taking the first step, then sinking down like a small, heavy stone. "You are asking all the wrong questions," said the fish, beginning to glow with an eerie blue light, "but I will tell you this last thing: Go down to the clearing near the marsh on the night of the full moon, and there you will find ten geese bigger than turkeys, and nine of them will have hummingbirds riding their backs, but the tenth will have a tiny saddle, and you must climb into it, and he will carry you very near to the edge of things.'' ''Hummingbirds?'' asked Toad, but the fish had already gone, leaving only a widening circle of silver, as if a shiny rock had been dropped into the black water, and then the moon went out, like a light.

Toad did as he was told, and on the night of the full moon, hopped down to the clearing by the marsh, and there were ten geese bigger than turkeys, and nine carried hummingbirds on their backs, but the tenth had a tiny saddle, empty. Toad climbed up as best he could, and with a great rustling like wind in the rushes, the geese rose into the air, fanning out, in a shape like a V. They flew over the forest, and over the black road with its white stripe down the center, which forked, like a skunk, and over houses with square yellow windows the color of moths in the meadow, and then over a black water without boundary or end, and the moon floated below like a plate, and fish leaped on it and off. ''Is this the edge of things?'' asked Toad, but the Goose would not answer; his great dark wings kept beating the dark air like fins, and looking back, Toad saw the other geese in a fan-shape behind him, beating their wings, black shapes the moon sketched in with silver. Finally, they flew over a shore so black it seemed a thickening of the water, and Toad felt the Goose beginning to sink like a leaf. ''Is this the edge of things?'' asked Toad, but the Goose would not answer, only tilted his neck toward the ground, and Toad slid down, as on the bannister of a stair. Silently, the geese rose into the air, their honking dimming as they faded slowly from sight, flakes of darkness, and finally, nothing at all.

Then Toad shook himself and looked around, and he could see the land around him dissolving like sand, and the stars were waiting like shells cast up by the tide, and when he looked again, they looked distinctly like crowns. ''The edge of things,'' murmured Toad to himself, wonderingly, and in the distance, he could see a great round dome, glowing blue-gray. ''The crown at the edge of things,'' said Toad, catching his breath, and setting off as fast as he could in the flickering gray light, while the stars seemed to be singing a strange song, but he could not understand, and the voice of the fish seemed to sound from the sky like a mysterious tide. Finally, Toad reached the dome, which was also a building, and saw the door was covered by a curtain of silk, at once solid and transparent as glass, and stuck all over with tiny white stars. "Now I will be King," said Toad to himself, hopping right in, asking no questions, looking neither to the left nor the right.

"Are you the King?" asked Toad, astonished, for in the center of the dome stood a great gnarled Tree, one arm holding the sun, the other the moon, and each twig a star. "I am the King," said the Tree, whose mouth was a gnarl where a branch had been broken, and the Tree began juggling the Sun, and the Moon, and the stars, silver balls, a gold ball, the North Star, the Dog Star, keeping them all in the air, none of them falling. "My!" said Toad, practically speechless, more amazed than before. "Can I try?" "Not just yet," said the Tree, twisting its bark of a mouth into a wrinkly smile. "What happens if one drops?" asked the Toad, curious. Then he heard the voice of the fish whispering *"yes, yes,"* and the Tree darkened with green blood, and stared at the wall straight behind him. Then Toad was chilly with fear, and turned, and looked, and saw a huge flaming stone falling onto a house, which turned red with spires, a red crown of flame, and heard dim cries, and saw the forest where the raccoon was attacking the cat, and the fisher-man hoisting a fish, lifting the lid of his basket, and the chip-munk running into the road, and under a great, spinning wheel. "Is that the answer?" whispered Toad in horror, but already he could feel his mouth forming the words, "That is the an-swer," and felt his arms moving upward to catch the great golden ball, and his toad flesh thickening and thickening into bark, while the balls flew into his hands more and more numerous than flies, and his eyes were riveted to the blank, staring wall.

"The edge of things, the edge of things!" cried Toad in despair, and as he watched, he saw the old King turning slowly into a lion with a great golden mane, twitching his last branch like a tail. "How long must I stay here?" cried Toad, his head

bent forward by the heavy gold crown. The Lion shook his head
sadly, and murmured of the edge of things, and temptations in
mirrors, or rivers, and the moon spinning in its tracks, and the
crown, hanging on the gray gray hook of time, and the Goose,
who came this way once, every two hundred years. Then his
eye gleamed like a jewel, and with a flick of his tail he was gone.

The Toad Who Didn't Know
What to Do

Once upon a time, there was an old woman named Celia, who lived with her husband Sam under the roots of a great, gnarled tree. Celia had no children at all, although she loved them quite dearly, and had wished for them on stars and on clover for many, many years. She tended to be absent-minded, and was usually to be found worrying about what she had just that minute lost. But during the day, while the sun shone brightly, like the dandelions that new mothers hung over the cribs of their babies to keep them from crying, she would sit in front of her easel in the short grass, which got browner and browner as it approached her front door. There she would paint little pictures of white animals with gold horns in their foreheads, and tiny elephants, flying like wasps on rainbow-hued wings, and rabbits in black suits and brocaded vests, playing checkers and chess.

Mothers of little toads hid in the bushes around Celia's house, and as the sun went down slowly, pulling in its petals, one at a time, they would try to hop up to her first, and the first mother to reach her would take the picture just finished home to her children, and it was said, at night, it came alive, and the creatures in it came and stood around the crib, or sat at the foot of the bed, moving their pawns and their kings, their horsemen and knights.

One day, while Celia was painting a new picture, using a sharp blade of grass for a brush, a very Old Wrinkled Toad hopped out of the forest, and over to her. "You are more wrinkled than last year's leaf," said Celia, laughing, putting down her brush, and clapping her hands. "How lucky you are, a year for each wrinkle, or crinkle, and yet, we can count them, without first chopping you down, like a tree." "I am very old," said the Old Wrinkled Toad, leaning on her stick, "and I have seen much, yet there is one thing I have not seen, and that is one of your pictures." "But you have no babies," said Celia, "and that is who they are for," bending over her canvas, drawing in a cloud speckled like the blue egg of a robin, and beginning to hatch. "Be that as it may," said the ancient toad, "I have many wrinkles, and may have what I will." "Well, you may certainly have it," said Celia, "for you are indeed wrinkled and ancient, and it may bring back the early days to you, when you were green as this grass, and some say the sun shone bright blue." "Blue as a sapphire it was, and the nights were all golden," the ancient one said, taking the picture, and beginning to hobble off, and as she got to the brink of the forest where she seemed a bit of gray tree trunk herself, she turned and said, "You will do no more crying in these dark ink-blue nights." Then the wife put down her brush, and stared after her into the forest, sightless, and when her husband hopped home from raking his leaves, she was sitting there still, stiller than stone.

Soon Celia began to notice that the other wives would come and stand at the edge of the forest, smiling, and then hop back into the shade, and although she painted her pictures faster and faster, and more and more fantastical, no one asked her for them, or would take them if offered, so she hung them all on the walls of their one empty room.

One night, when they were sleeping, Celia had a curious dream. All the little creatures in the house were getting out of their pictures and were busying themselves with something in the corner of the room she could not see at all. The unicorn seemed to be stirring something with his sharp, golden horn, and the tiny elephants were flying through the air, their mouths full of white roses. When Celia woke up again, it was still dark, but there it was, right in the middle of the room, luminous, as the moon, a great wedding cake! And there on the top were two figures, perfect likenesses of herself and her husband, but looking much younger, made out of sugar, and a long crystally veil swirled over her shoulders, and over their toad feet, and glinted in the moonlight like cold snow. Then the cake turned, and she could see it was cut in half, and hinged, and made up of tiny apartments, just like a beehive, and in one, the unicorn was bathing in a marble tubful of milk, and in the others, tiny children were sleeping, the frames of her pictures on their walls, tiny windows, but their occupants were all out of their frames, nodding at the foot of the beds. "Curious," said Celia, dropping off to sleep.

But in the morning, she told her husband about it, and he solemnly told her that they must first build her a rocker, and it must be built out of the old blades of grass she used for her brushes, and since Sam was wise in the meanings of dreams, this is just what they did. They wove the brushes into plaits for the runners, and took little buckets of sap from the trees, and coated the runners with them, until they were solid and thick, then the backs of the chair, and the arms. Then they stood back holding paws. "Good!" said the husband, and that night, they both had a strange dream.

Little creatures were spinning spider webs out of sugar, and pasting on silver sequins they carried down from the sky, and which glittered like snow, and as each strand hardened, it wove into the most remarkable carriage they ever had seen. Then they thought they saw the crinkly lady, and heard a shrill cry, and then in the morning, waking up, they were astounded to find it was still there, the sun shining through it, bright bones of glass, and in its center, under a coverlet of roses, a tiny new baby, looking just like Celia and Sam.

Celia, who had not cried for many months now, went to get it something to eat ("Fly pudding, fly pudding!" she sang out happily, hopping off to the kitchen), and Sam thought the sun looked unusually blue for that time of day, and blessed his good fortune, although for the first week, he could not quite believe it, and pinched his arm so many times to make sure he was not dreaming, it ended quite swollen and sore, and they called him Fred.

But he was a wonder! Immediately, Sam and Celia began to discuss what he would be. But the more they thought, the more they could not decide, since the little toad child seemed as various as the great, cloudy sky, every minute altering. Finally, the little toad grew into a handsome, small boy, and they began to discuss the matter with him (it was his favorite topic, better than any story of witches or bears), but what would he be?

Would he perhaps be a fireman? Firemen were much respected in Toadland, where every house was in a tree, and every tree made of wood. But Celia, who had held him for hours in front of their fire, where he had watched flames flicker and dance, said "Oh, but he would not like to put them out, when they dance up so high!" "True," said little Fred, "they dance into the sky like a castle of flame, full of spires, a great, orange crown." "Well, then, a poet," Sam suggested, catching something in the phrasing he liked very much. "But he should have no money!" wailed his mother, and Fred agreed he loved his allowance, with which he bought crayons and paint and toy trains. "Perhaps in his spare time, then," Sam said, puckering his forehead. "A plumber!" Celia exclaimed, but Fred thought, and said, on the whole, he preferred dry leaves to wet, for he had a dislike of white mushrooms that kept clogging the pipes in wet weather. "They seem so like creatures, too," he said, "little soldiers in helmets; I would not care to touch them." "A doctor?" his mother suggested, hopeful. "The boy is of a delicate nature," Sam interjected, "and if someone took ill, they would bury him instead of the patient." "I *would* think it my fault," piped up Fred very solemn. "A student?" suggested Celia. "I *do* so like books," Fred said, sitting up straighter, then standing, and giving a hop. "Then you will be a student," said Sam, relieved and final. "Though pages are quite like mushrooms, especially in the winter," Fred said uneasily, but in spite of these misgivings, the matter was closed.

So Fred began to study. He started with A : anthropologist.

"They say we are descended from the tree or the tree leaf," he told his amazed mother, taking her out in the yard, and pointing to her arm to the tree flesh and tree leaf. "They say next I must go dig for bones; it is very important," Fred told her, squeamish. "I think I must go on to the B's: botanist." "This is very depressing," Fred said, some weeks later, showing Sam his new book, "there are annuals and perennials, but something gets them all in the end. I think I will go on to the C's: chemist."

By now, Sam and Celia were getting quite old, and moving quite slowly, so sometimes, to them, the sun seemed to run through the sky. One morning, after an explosion had rocked the little house under the tree trunk, and smashed a sugar-pane window, Celia and Sam went to see Fred, who had reached D for dentist. "Detestable drill, the noise is quite deafening," he complained the minute he saw them. "We should like to see you get to Z," said Sam, "but I am afraid we are getting to D ourselves—death." "But death is *very* unpleasant," objected Fred. "You become hard as a rock, and cannot move, anymore than a stone, and never speak, until the sun rolls out of the sky like a stone." "I am afraid we have let it be chosen for us," said Celia. "It will be as it must." "Foolish," said Fred, shaking his head, raising his voice over the noise of the drill, for he could not understand this news at all, but the next week, they were rigid as stone, and as Fred has just passed through F for florist, he now entered G for grief, arranging garlands about their heads and feet, and choking with groans.

The years passed, and Fred reached R for ranger, and watched the town from a high tree, and then V for voyager, and made many trips, but no place seemed quite like his village, so he always came home, and finally he reached Z for zippers, but they stuck far too frequently for his taste, and by now his hands were arthritic. "Everyone should wear capes," was his solemn advice to those who came to his shop. "I will begin again with the A's," he said to himself: "anthropologist, actor, this time, I will make automobiles." But his sight was so foggy, he forgot the third wheel and drove straight into a tree, and walked around for days, turbaned like a turk. One day, Death himself drove by, and heard Fred musing: "Blitzkrieg Director," he was saying to himself. "What next?" thought Death, laughing, which for him was a rare thing, and so left him alone. "Billiard parlor and cues, two in one," he heard Fred musing as he next passed by, and Death laughed till he shook. "Bail bondsman," he heard next, as he went about his rounds, "but then, I have a distinct dislike for criminals." Fred ruminated again through his beard: "Clocks, gingerbread," he pronounced at last. Death could hardly believe it, for Fred was getting too deaf to hear if clocks ticked, much less struck the hours. "Artificial cats, or perhaps caskets!" he heard, passing again, "ceilings or cellars!" But by this time, Death was beginning to tire of him, and began skipping his house when he passed by. "Xylophones!" he thought he heard one day, and Death looked at his watch and hurried on; *his* job, he thought to himself, was not really so bad. Just this morning, the wrinkled lady had called him twice, quite as if he were a taxicab, and as he carried her off in his arms, light as a leaf, smiling with gratitude, he thought he could hear "chimneys and bricks!" in Fred's ancient quaver.

So Death forgot him, and eventually, as Anthropology had prophecied, Fred began to grow so old he resembled the gray tree flesh he lived in, and was more wrinkled than the old wrinkled lady ("Accordion!" he gasped out, waked from a dream) and eventually became the wonder of the town to whom he was older than the sun, but no wiser than the leaf flesh he now so perfectly resembled.

One day, a mother brought her child to him; the child stared and stared. "A fireman, mommy!" he shrieked, snatching a helmet out of her shopping bag and dashing back into the town. The next morning, another mother arrived with her daughter. "A doctor!" the child screamed, throwing down her palette, and fastening her stethoscope around her neck like a necklace. And so it went on, whenever a mind hovered like a fly between two flowers, and, though now no one knows which, there is still a tree which can be heard, on quiet nights only, saying "Postage!" or "Squirrels!" or "Mansions," or "Laundry!" or "Streetcars!" and though desperate mothers occasionally venture out with their children ("Rubbish! Sweaters! Tinker Toys! Underwear! Valentines!"), Death himself shuns the place.

21 DAY BOOK